To my family

www.hungrymanbooks.com
Contact the author at: oren_ginzburg@yahoo.com

First published March 2005
This edition published June 2006
Also available in Spanish and Italian

ISBN 0 946592 22 5

Printed on Sappi Paper by Mediaprint

With special thanks to Violaine and Noa!

Foreword

'There you go!' is an arrow defending tribal peoples. In my 33 years with Survival, I have not come across anything else that hits the bull's eye with such simplicity, accuracy and irrepressible humour. Today the subject of tribal peoples and development is saturated with words, but if you really want to understand what's going on, read this book.

The 'development' of tribal peoples against their wishes – really to let others get their land and resources – is rooted in 19th century colonialism ('we know best') dressed up in 20th century 'politically correct' euphemism. Tribal peoples are not backward: they are independent and vibrant societies which, like all of us always, are constantly adapting to a changing world. The main difference between tribal peoples and us is that we take their land and resources, and believe the dishonest, even racist, claim that it's for their own good. It's conquest, not development.

Survival International helps tribal peoples defend their lives, protect their lands and determine their own futures. We are delighted to have the opportunity to give Oren's book to tribal communities around the world, as well as to governments and others who should know better and who must stop living in the past.

Stephen Corry
Director, Survival International, 2006

Our original aim was the same as usual:

to bring them sustainable development.

However, in this specific case

we encountered an unexpected challenge.

It turns out that these people,

in their own strange kind of way,

were already sustainable.

So all we could really bring them was...

Development.

We started with Participatory Community Development...

but they did not fully participate.

We tried income-generating activities... but some people seem satisfied with less than a dollar a day.

We even attempted to empower them... but
their reaction was more powerful than expected.

So we opted for a Multi-Stakeholder Cross-Disciplinary Integrated approach.

We developed innovative
Private Sector Partnerships.

We developed Vocational Skills
adapted to a shifting economy.

We developed tough conservation measures,
to protect the environment from further harm.

And we developed ambitious Social Safety Nets
– for those unable to take care of themselves.

This has been a challenging process
with many lessons learned.

We certainly look forward to applying them elsewhere in the very near future.

But for now let us just say,

Welcome to the Global Village!

There you go, again

The destruction of tribal peoples in the name of 'development' – invariably because outsiders want their land and its resources – continues to be the most acute problem they face. It is not confined to poor countries.

In Canada, the Innu Indians of Labrador and Quebec have been settled in communities which are subject to the 'development' depicted in 'There you go!'. The Innu were self-sufficient as recently as the 1960s. Now, very few hunt the caribou or fish the lakes they once depended on. Grossly insensitive schooling, total dependency on welfare programmes and the resulting abject poverty have largely destroyed their way of life and demolished their self-esteem. Domestic violence and the cheapest forms of drug abuse – gas sniffing and alcoholism – are rife. Some communities have the highest suicide rate in the world and every family knows at least one teenager who has killed him or herself.

Canada says it will negotiate about their land rights, but only once the Indians have abandoned them. It is no accident that Innu territory includes some of the world's richest nickel deposits. The Innu have not given up: they are struggling to fight back, but they face powerful odds and grossly out-of-date prejudice.

Fighting back!

The future for tribal peoples doesn't have to be as depicted in this book.

In the 1970s one of the largest Amazonian tribes, the Yanomami, was threatened by the dismemberment of its land to make way for Brazil's road programme. Despite the international campaign Survival launched to defend the Indians, about 20% of Yanomami tragically died from diseases brought in by gold miners.

The campaign was victorious in 1992, when all Yanomami land was secured. Although their problems are not over, the Indians now have their own organisation to press for their rights. In some communities, children are learning from their own teachers and in their own schools how to cope with outside threats. The Yanomami remain true to the best of their traditions. They do not see themselves as poor or backward, and can expect to lead fulfilling lives – as Yanomami – for generations to come.

For more information on threatened tribal peoples and how you can help, please contact:

Survival International (head office)
6 Charterhouse Buildings
London EC1M 7ET, UK

Survival also has offices in France, Germany, Italy and Spain.

T +44 (0) 20 7687 8700

info@survival-international.org
www.survival-international.org

Roy Sesana GANA BUSHMAN, BOTSWANA

'I SAY WHAT KIND OF DEVELOPMENT IS
IT WHEN THE PEOPLE LIVE SHORTER LIVES
THAN BEFORE? THEY CATCH HIV/AIDS. OUR
CHILDREN ARE BEATEN IN SCHOOL AND
WON'T GO. SOME BECOME PROSTITUTES.
THEY ARE NOT ALLOWED TO HUNT. THEY
FIGHT BECAUSE THEY ARE BORED AND
GET DRUNK. THEY ARE STARTING TO
COMMIT SUICIDE. WE NEVER SAW THAT
BEFORE. IS THIS 'DEVELOPMENT'?'

SEND 'THERE YOU GO!' TO A FRIEND

We think this book should be circulated as widely as possible. **CAN YOU HELP?**

If you know anyone who would be interested in receiving a copy of 'There you go!',
or indeed someone who helps shape the 'development' policies which affect tribal
peoples, please let us know.

If you are able to, please ensure your donation covers our minimum print and postage
costs. The suggested donation to Survival is £5.00 per copy. Please use the donation
form provided overleaf. **THANK YOU.**

I would like Survival to send 'There you go!' to:

FIRST COPY

First name	Last name	BLOCK CAPITALS PLEASE
Position (if applicable)		
Address		
Postcode	Country	

SECOND COPY

First name	Last name	BLOCK CAPITALS PLEASE
Position (if applicable)		
Address		
Postcode	Country	

HAVE YOUR SAY

We would like to know what you think about the issues raised in this book.
Please send us your comments, using the space below.

I WANT TO HELP TRIBAL PEOPLES

First name	Last name	BLOCK CAPITALS PLEASE

Address

Postcode	Country

Email

STANDING ORDER FORM (UK only)

You can cancel a standing order at any time by notifying us and your bank/building society.

Bank/building society name

Bank/building society address

Postcode

Please pay Survival *(tick chosen amount or fill in other amount)*:

£3	other £	**each month**	Account no.
£8	other £	**each quarter**	Sort code
£25	other £	**each year**	Signature
Starting on / /			Date

This is **in addition to** / **replaces** (please delete as appropriate) any existing standing order to Survival.

AND/OR I WISH TO MAKE A GIFT OF:

£250	£100	£50	£25	other £

Additional donation for extra copies of **'There you go!'** £

☐ I enclose a cheque made payable to **'Survival'**

☐ I wish to pay by Visa/MasterCard/Switch/Maestro/CAF Card/Delta/JCB/Eurocard. Number:

													switch only	switch only	switch only

valid from   expiry date   switch issue no.

security number   Signature:

☐ Please reclaim the tax on all my donations to Survival International made since 6 April 2001 and any I make from now on. *You must pay an amount of UK income or capital gains tax at least equal to the tax we reclaim on your donations (currently 28p for every £1 you give).* *giftaid it*

Please return this form to:

SURVIVAL, FREEPOST PAM 5410, LONDON EC1B 1EE, UK
No postage required if posted in UK. Do not return to your bank/building society.

To keep costs down, we do not normally send acknowledgments of gifts. Please tick if you require one. ☐

For official use: To Bank of Scotland, West End Office, St James' Gate, 14/16 Cockspur St, London, SW1Y 5BL, Survival International Charitable Trust (12-11-03) A/C 00768011, quoting the customer's name and our reference. **Survival will not pass on any of your details to any other organisation.**

OUR REF: